Kids Taking Action
READING COMPREHENSION
Real Kids Making Real Changes

Grades 5–6

CR 9105

Author
Tracy Edmunds, M.A. Ed.

Managing Editor
Mara Ellen Guckian

Editor in Chief
Brent L. Fox, M. Ed.

Creative Director
Sarah M. Fournier

Cover Artist
Diem Pascarella

Art Coordinator
Renée Mc Elwee

Illustrator
Renée Mc Elwee

Imaging
Crystal-Dawn Keitz

Publisher
Mary D. Smith, M.S. Ed.

Teacher Created Resources
12621 Western Avenue
Garden Grove, CA 92841
www.teachercreated.com

ISBN: 978-1-4206-1711-5

©2022 Teacher Created Resources

Made in U.S.A.

For standards correlations, visit
http://www.teachercreated.com/standards/

Teacher Created Resources

Table of Contents

Introduction	3
How to Use This Book	3
Community Investigation	5
Vocabulary List	7
Vocabulary Graphic Organizer	9
Taking Action	10
Unit 1: Ryan Hickman	12
Unit 2: Jayera Griffin	18
Unit 3: Katie Stagliano	24
Unit 4: Shanneil Turner	30
Unit 5: Sidney Keys III	36
Unit 6: Lesein Mutunkei	42
Unit 7: Janine Licare and Aislin Livingstone	48
Unit 8: Salvador Gómez-Colón	54
Unit 9: Areeta Wong	60
Unit 10: Jaylen Arnold	66
Unit 11: Jordan Reeves	72
Motto Bookmarks	78
Bibliography	79

Introduction

Kids of all ages are eager to help build a better world. They see problems, in school and out. Many are concerned about both their immediate situations and their futures. They want to know what they can do to help.

Research shows that helping others relieves anxiety, reduces stress, improves mood, boosts self-esteem, and instills a sense of purpose and satisfaction. Taking positive actions can help kids cope with their fears and become informed, active citizens in their communities.

The informational texts in this book present examples of positive activism initiated by young people. The kids in these texts are "everyday people" making a difference in their communities through positive activism related to their environments, their education, and their desire to help people in need. They put their imaginations and optimism to work and truly make a difference. Their examples encourage students to find positive solutions and show them that their age is not a barrier to becoming forces for positive change.

> "Young people, when they understand a problem, are empowered to take action. When we listen to their voices (they) actually are changing the world and making it better for people, for animals, and for the environment because everything is interconnected."—Jane Goodall

How to Use This Book

Community Investigation

Start by discussing the concept of community. Use the *Community Investigation* pages (5–6) to have students research and learn more about the communities they are a part of. Depending on how deeply students delve into their communities, this activity could take days or even weeks. Once students have an established sense of their own communities, it is time to share units about students in other communities and explore what they have accomplished. You may wish to choose a unit based on student interest, or just start at the beginning and do them all!

Informational Text Units

Each six-page unit for informational text learning is set up in the same manner to provide consistency for students. Each unit includes the following components:

- **Nonfiction Passage.** Each two-page nonfiction passage features a young person who spots a need in their community and decides to do something about it. These nonfiction texts include a variety of text features to enhance students' understanding and draw attention to important facts. They include subheads, quotes, bold-faced words, sidebars and insets, vocabulary callouts, and footnotes. Students can read the texts individually or in groups, and they are perfect for repeated readings.

How to Use This Book (cont.)

⌘ **Text Questions.** The three pages of text questions each focus on different nonfiction reading skills:

- *Key Ideas and Details* questions ask students to identify what the text says, including main idea and key details.
- *Craft and Structure* questions focus on the author's craft and organizational patterns, including vocabulary.
- *Integration of Knowledge and Meaning* questions focus on analyzing what the text means, and they also integrate new information with students' own knowledge and experiences.

⌘ **Culminating Unit Activities.** The final page of each unit helps students consolidate the knowledge they have accumulated and consider ways they might put it to use.

- *Group Discussion* questions help students connect the ideas in the text to their own lives and communities and possibly implement them with adult supervision. These can be used for either small-group or whole-group discussion.
- *Taking Action* asks students to apply the ideas in the text to a problem in their own communities. These activities help students understand how collaborating in their communities can help them to be part of solutions.

Vocabulary

Some vocabulary words are defined in callouts within the texts. A more extensive vocabulary list is included on pages 7–8, along with a graphic organizer on page 9 for students to think about word meanings from multiple angles.

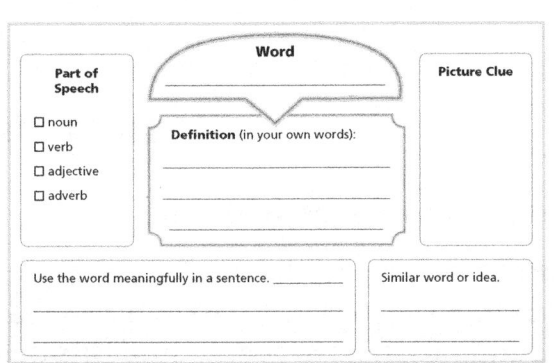

Take Action in Your Community

As a culminating activity, have students use the *Take Action* activity (pages 10–11) to plan and carry out positive actions.

- In Part 1, students choose a community and define a problem through research and dialogue with community members.
- In Part 2, they make a plan for action and put it into practice. Students may want to take action individually, in small groups, or even as a project for the entire class.
- In Part 3, students reflect on what they have learned and consider what they might do next.

Note to Teacher: As students plan their projects, consider any safety issues and work with them to create a workable plan.

Community Investigation

Name: _____ Date: _____

Part 1: Defining *Your* Community

> ➡ *What is a community?*
> - a particular area where a group of people live
> - a group of people who live or work close together or have shared interests
> - a feeling of fellowship (belonging) with others as a result of sharing common attitudes, interests, and goals

1. What type of community do you live in?

   ☐ Urban ☐ Suburban ☐ Rural ☐ Other: _____

   What is the population? _____

2. Check off the local communities you feel most connected to. Add more if necessary.

   ☐ Family   ☐ Online community   ☐ Country
   ☐ Classroom   ☐ Volunteer community   ☐ World
   ☐ School   ☐ Neighborhood   ☐ _____
   ☐ Religious community   ☐ Town or city   ☐ _____
   ☐ Club or scouts community ☐ State or region   ☐ _____

3. Choose one of your communities to focus on. _____

4. Describe your community.

   Who is part of this community? _____
   _____

   Where do you interact? _____

   What do you have in common? _____

   How are you different from one another? _____

5. What does this community do for you? _____
   _____

©Teacher Created Resources #9105 Kids Taking Action

Community Investigation *(cont.)*

Name: _____ Date: _____

Part 2: Community Issues and Needs

1. What are some needs you have seen in your community?
   _____

2. What resources already exist in your community? Look for people, places, and organizations that provide information and help to community members. **Example:** In many communities, the public library is an important source of information.

People	Places	Organizations
Who are they? _____	Where are they? _____	What are they? _____
What do they do to help? _____ _____	What do they do to help? _____ _____	What do they do to help? _____ _____

3. Have you seen or been a part of community-service projects?   **Yes**   **Not yet**

   If yes, what worked? _____
   _____

   What didn't work as well? _____

4. If you put together a project to help your community, who could you ask for help?
   _____
   _____

5. What laws, rules, or customs should you be aware of? _____
   _____

Vocabulary List

acre—a unit of area equal to 43,560 square feet, about the size of a football field

activism—taking action to make change

affectionately—in a way that shows care or love

appreciate—to see the worth of something

biodegradable—able to be broken down by living things

bully—to purposely hurt, intimidate, threaten, or ridicule someone, especially repeatedly

captions—text on a screen that shows what is being said

certified—officially recognized as possessing certain qualifications

chapters—groups or clubs

coding—writing script in a language that a computer can understand

collaborate—to work together

community—a group of people with common interests

community service—volunteer work to help a large number of people in a particular area or location

crowdfunding—raising money through small donations from a lot of people, usually through a website

cyberbullying—the use of electronic communication for bullying

deaf—unable to hear or have difficulty hearing

deforestation—the action of clearing a wide area of trees to make room for farms and grazing animals or to obtain wood for fuel and construction

devastated—destroyed or ruined

diagnose—observe symptoms to decide what is causing a problem and what can be done to help

distribute/distribution—to give out or deliver

donate/donation/donating—giving help to people in need; to make a gift; to contribute to a cause

ecosystem—a home for many different types of plants and animals that depend on one another to live

empathy—the ability to imagine and understand the feelings of others; the act of being aware and understanding the feelings and thoughts of another person or group

environmentalist—someone who is concerned about the natural world and works to protect it

executive—a person who manages or directs; someone who directs or controls a company

exotic—a plant or animal brought in from another place

fantasy—a work of literature set in an unreal world often with superhuman characters and monsters

food insecurity—inability to find or get healthy food

frequented—visited often

generator—a machine that produces electricity

grant—a gift of money to be used for a specific purpose

grassroots—starting with or coming from everyday people

habitat fragmentation—when an area is split up into sections by roads, buildings, or other structures so that animals cannot safely travel between them to get to food, water, and their homes

hackathon—an event where people work together using technology to solve a problem

Vocabulary List (cont.)

hacker—a person who can program and solve problems with a computer

immune system—a system in the body that protects it from infection

inclusive design—creating places and things that are usable by everyone

indigenous—produced, growing, or living naturally in a particular region or environment

internship—working for a short time with a company or organization to learn new skills

launch—start; introduce; open

mentor—a person who teaches or gives help and advice to a less experienced and often younger person

motivated—having interest or enthusiasm for doing something

native—something that lives or grows naturally in a region

partner—to work together

predicament—a difficult, unpleasant, or embarrassing situation

prevent—to keep from happening

prosthetic—a specially created body part, such as an arm, a foot, or a tooth, that replaces a missing part

publisher—company that sells books, newspapers, or magazines

ration—use in small amounts; use for a short amount of time

recyclables—items that can be used again or can be used to make other products

recyle—turn waste into reusable material

reforest—plant tree seeds or young trees in an area where there used to be a forest

rehabilitate—provide care to sick, injured, and orphaned wild animals so they can be returned to their natural habitat

sanctuary—a place where animals are brought to live and be protected

saplings—young trees

scholarship—money given to support a person's academic or athletic future

self-conscious—uncomfortably aware of oneself being observed by others

soup kitchen—a place that serves free food to needy people

sponsor—a person or a company that pays for a project

STEM—science, technology, engineering, and math

stereotype—to believe unfairly that all people or things with a particular characteristic are the same

tics—uncontrollable body movements or vocal sounds

traditional—following ideas and practices of the past

tutoring—giving instruction or academic help to an individual

volunteerism—the act of doing volunteer work

voucher—printed paper or card that allows the holder (person) to exchange it for goods or services

vowed—promised

wearables—any kind of electronic device designed to be worn on the user's body

workshop—a small group or class formed to learn new skills

Vocabulary Graphic Organizer

Name: _____ Date: _____

Word
_____

Part of Speech
☐ noun
☐ verb
☐ adjective
☐ adverb

Definition (in your own words):
_____
_____
_____

Picture Clue

Use the word meaningfully in a sentence. _____
_____
_____

Similar word or idea.
_____
_____

Word
_____

Part of Speech
☐ noun
☐ verb
☐ adjective
☐ adverb

Definition (in your own words):
_____
_____
_____

Picture Clue

Use the word meaningfully in a sentence. _____
_____
_____

Similar word or idea.
_____
_____

©Teacher Created Resources

Taking Action

Name: _____ Date: _____

Part 1: The Problem

1. What community will you focus on?
   _____

2. Who are the members of this community?
   _____
   _____

3. What need or issue will you address?
   _____
   _____

4. **Research** to learn more about the issue.

   What is the issue? _____

   Who is involved? _____

   When and where do things take place? _____

   Why is this an issue? _____
   _____

5. **Listen** to others, and talk with them about the issue.

   Who is affected? _____

   How can you connect with the people involved to find out what would be helpful?
   _____

   What do they say the problem is? _____

   What do they think would help? _____
   _____

Taking Action *(cont.)*

Name: _____ **Date:** _____

Part 2: Take Action

1. **Define and share** your own ideas.

   What is the specific problem? _____
   _____

   What are your ideas for solutions? _____
   _____

   How can you share these ideas with those who are affected? _____
   _____

   How can you share these ideas with those who can make change? _____
   _____

2. **Take action** to address the issue.

   What is your plan of action? _____
   _____

   What is the first step? _____
   _____

Part 3: Reflect

1. **Reflect** on what you have learned about working with your community to accomplish your projects (goals).
   _____

2. What can you do for your community moving forward? _____
   _____

©Teacher Created Resources   #9105 Kids Taking Action

Unit 1
Ryan Hickman

Ryan Recycles

When Ryan Hickman was just three years old, he went with his dad to their local recycling center. They turned in some bags full of empty bottles and cans. Ryan really liked it! He liked it so much that he told his parents he wanted to ask their neighbors to save cans and bottles so he could turn them in, too.

They got some bags and passed them out to their neighbors. Ryan asked them to save empty plastic and glass bottles and aluminum cans in the bags. Once a week, Ryan and his dad collected the bags. They took them to the recycling center. In California, where Ryan lives, people can turn in **recyclables** and get a few cents for each can or bottle. Ryan got a little bit of money. He decided to save money so that someday he could buy a full-size garbage truck.

"Ryan's Recycling" grew and grew. More people collected recyclables for him. Businesses and schools started collecting, too. Ryan and his dad were taking truckloads of bottles and cans to the collection center every week.[1]

Helping Ocean Animals

One day, Ryan's family was visiting their local beach. Ryan noticed that there was trash everywhere. He knew that trash on the beach can easily get into the ocean. Ocean animals can get hurt or die. They can get tangled up in the trash. They eat trash, and it makes them sick or kills them.

Ryan decided to clean up the beach! He kept the bottles and cans for recycling and put the other trash into trash cans. Ryan loved cleaning up the beach. He invited people to clean up beaches with him. Now, Ryan and his parents hold beach cleanup days whenever they can. Many people come to help. Ryan gives them buckets to put trash in. He sets up a place where they can bring the trash and sort out the recyclables. He and his family got their **community** involved. One business helped by **donating** buckets. Another business donated tools to pick up the trash.

Recycling

To **recycle** means to turn something old into something new. Things that can be recycled include plastic, glass, and aluminum. These things can be melted down and used to make new products. Sometimes, they are used to make new cans and bottles. They can also be used to make new things like clothing, plastic bags, and even playgrounds.

Recycling helps the environment because:

- it keeps trash out of the environment and landfills
- it saves the resources and energy that would be used to make new bottles and cans

---

1. Capo Dispatch. "Recycling Advocate Ryan Hickman, 11, Finalist for 'TIME's' Kid of the Year Award," *The Capistrano Dispatch*, November 25, 2020.

Ryan Hickman (cont.)

Care for Injured Ocean Animals

Ryan wanted to do more to help ocean animals. He visited a place that helps seals and sea lions that are hurt. They **rehabilitate** the seals and sea lions and release them back into the ocean when they are better. Ryan wanted to raise money to help the animal-care center. He started selling T-shirts and hats with fun pictures and sayings on them like, "Make the Sea Trash Free." Ryan's parents help him sell the shirts and hats online. People have bought them from as far away as India and South Africa. Ryan gives all the money he makes from selling T-shirts to the rehabilitation center. It helps pay for medicine and food for the sea animals. Ryan likes to deliver the money in person and visit the seals and sea lions.

Making a Difference

Ryan still loves recycling. After school and on weekends, he and his dad go around and collect recyclables. At 11 years old, he has collected over one million cans and bottles! Ryan talks to people all over the world to tell them how important it is to recycle and help the environment.

> "It's really easy to make a difference," Ryan said. "I always tell people to try your best to recycle what you use every day, and if you see a piece of trash on the ground, please pick it up and throw it away. I'm only 11 years old. If I can make a difference, you can, too."[2]

How Can You Recycle?

First, check which items can be recycled where you live. Not all plastic can be recycled, so look for the recycle symbol. Once you have collected recyclables, sort the different kinds of materials. Put all the aluminum together, all the glass together, and all the plastic together.

Some places ask people to sort their recycling at home. It is picked up by a truck and taken to a recycling center. In other places, people take the recyclables to special centers themselves.

2. Capo Dispatch. "Recycling Advocate Ryan Hickman, 11, Finalist for 'TIME's' Kid of the Year Award," *The Capistrano Dispatch*, November 25, 2020.

Unit 1

Name: _____ Date: _____

Key Ideas and Details

Directions: Answer the questions below about Ryan Hickman. Use complete sentences.

1. What is the main idea of this text? How do you know?

   _____

   _____

   _____

   _____

2. How does recycling help the environment? Cite text evidence.

   _____

   _____

   _____

   _____

   _____

3. Where does Ryan get the cans and bottles he recycles?

   _____

   _____

   _____

   _____

   _____

4. Who helps Ryan with recycling? What do they do to help him?

   _____

   _____

   _____

   _____

   _____

Name: _____ **Date:** _____

Craft and Structure

Directions: Answer the questions below. Use complete sentences.

1. What does the word *rehabilitate* mean? How is it used in this text?

   _____
   _____
   _____
   _____
   _____

2. How does the section "Helping Ocean Animals" help you understand more about Ryan?

   _____
   _____
   _____
   _____
   _____

3. Why do you think the author included the quote by Ryan?

   _____
   _____
   _____
   _____
   _____
   _____

Unit 1

Name: _____ **Date:** _____

Integration of Knowledge and Meaning

Directions: Answer the questions below. Use complete sentences.

1. What does the recycling logo help you understand about recycling?

   _____
   _____
   _____
   _____
   _____

2. The author says that Ryan likes recycling. What evidence does the author give to support this?

   _____
   _____
   _____
   _____
   _____

3. How might this text be different if it had been written from Ryan's point of view?

   _____
   _____
   _____
   _____
   _____

Name: _____   Date: _____

Group Discussion

Brainstorming: Why did Ryan and his dad want people to help them? What did they ask people to do? How did they make it easier for people to help?

Taking Action

Directions: Everyone needs help sometimes! Think of a problem you have seen in your community, and answer the questions.

What could you do about it on your own?	
What would you need help with?	
How could you ask other people to help?	
What could you do to make it easier for them to help?	

Unit 2
Jayera Griffin

A Good Idea

Fourteen-year-old Jayera Griffin noticed a problem. When she was **tutoring** younger students, she saw that some of the kids' clothes were not as clean as they could be. She could tell that these kids were **self-conscious** about their appearance. Jayera worried that they would be made fun of. She thought that **bullying** would make it hard for them to learn.

Jayera asked her mom why kids might not have clean clothes to wear. Her mother told her that not everyone can afford a washer and a dryer at home. And some families can't afford to use the appliances in their apartment building. Some cannot get to the local laundromat as often as they would like. Jayera asked if she could help by washing kids' clothes for them. Her mom said she didn't think they could manage that much laundry. She asked Jayera to think of a better way to help.

Jayera had an idea. She saved her $5 a week allowance. She also asked for donations from friends and neighbors. She raised almost $1,000 and planned a Free Wash Day at the local coin laundry. First, she asked the laundromat owners for permission. Then, she made flyers. She handed them out around her school and neighborhood to tell people about the event.

➠ **self-conscious**—uncomfortably aware of oneself being observed by others

Free Wash Day

On Free Wash Day, Jayera fed quarters into the washers and dryers. Many people came to do their laundry. Jayera felt proud of how she was helping members of her community.

Jayera's Free Wash Day was a success! The Clorox® company heard about it. They contacted Jayera and offered to **sponsor** three more Free Wash Days! They paid for the free washes and donated laundry supplies. The mayor of Jayera's town proclaimed a Free Community Wash Day. The idea has now spread to other communities. They are offering their own free wash days.

➠ **sponsor**—a person, company, or organization that pays for a project or an event

Jayera Griffin (cont.)

More Ways to Help

Jayera's Free Wash Days were so successful that she looked for other ways to help people in her local community. Over the next few years, she tackled many more projects:

- She raised money to buy fire extinguishers and smoke detectors for seniors.
- She wanted to start a book club. She wrote to the local news station to ask if they could help get copies of books. The television station contacted **publishers**. They sent stacks of books.
- She raised funds to sponsor a CPR and first-aid class. Eleven people in the community became **certified** to do CPR. They can now help during emergencies.
- She saw that many students ran out of school supplies as the school year went on. She raised $1,000 to donate school supplies to her school district.
- She **partnered** with a roller-skating club. Together, they offered free skating one night a week at the local rink. Families could have some safe fun together.

Community service is important to Jayera's family. She started helping others when she was just two years old! Her mother took Jayara to volunteer at the local food bank. Little Jayera put cans of food into paper bags for families in need. Over time, she took on more and more responsibility. Eventually, she had her own table of bags to fill.

The Right Thing to Do

Jayera helps her community because she enjoys it. She also sees it as the right thing to do. Her **activism** has been noticed and honored. Her school district gave her the Spirit of Kindness award. The mayor of her town proclaimed Jayera Griffin Day! Jayera was also honored by Marvel as a Marvel Hero. They made a comic about her called "Radiant Jayera."

> What would Jayera say to other kids who want to help their communities?
>
> "I would tell them not to let anyone tell you that you can't do it. Because their opinion really doesn't matter when it comes to something that will help somebody else."[1]

1. Mason, Heather. "14-year-old Jayera Griffin is Working with Clorox to Provide Free Laundry Days to Her Community," June 22, 2018.

Unit 2

Name: _____ **Date:** _____

Key Ideas and Details

Directions: Answer the questions below about Jayera Griffin. Use complete sentences.

1. What made Jayera want to create Free Wash Day?

   _____

   _____

   _____

2. How did Jayera feel on her first Free Wash Day? Have you ever felt this way? Explain.

   _____

   _____

   _____

   _____

3. What details of Jayera's story stand out to you? Why?

   _____

   _____

   _____

   _____

4. What else would you like to learn about Jayera Griffin?

   _____

   _____

   _____

   _____

Unit 2

Name: _____ Date: _____

Craft and Structure

Directions: Answer the questions below. Use complete sentences.

1. What is the big idea you think the author wanted you to understand in this text?

   _____
   _____
   _____

2. Why do you think the author chose to use bullet points to list Jayera's other projects?

   _____
   _____

   How did the bullet points help you understand the text?

   _____
   _____
   _____

3. Choose one word from the text that you think is important to understanding Jayera's story. Define the word and explain its importance to the story.

   Word: _____

   Definition: _____
   _____
   _____

   Importance to the story: _____
   _____
   _____
   _____

Unit 2

Name: _____ Date: _____

Integration of Knowledge and Meaning

Directions: Answer the questions below. Use complete sentences.

1. Jayera worried that kids would be bullied because their clothes weren't clean. She thought that they would not be able to focus on their schoolwork. What are some other reasons kids might not be able to focus?

   _____
   _____
   _____
   _____
   _____

2. Look for patterns. What do you think all of Jayera's projects have in common?

   _____
   _____
   _____
   _____
   _____

3. Community service is important to Jayera's family. List some things that are important to your family.

   _____
   _____
   _____
   _____
   _____

Name: _____ Date: _____

Unit 2

Group Discussion

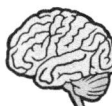

Brainstorming: Jayera raised money to help address needs in her community. What else did she do to get assistance for her causes?

Taking Action

Directions: Start a list on the back of this page of ways to generate help in a community. Include ideas that do not require you to raise money. What people or groups would you approach for assistance? How would you approach them? Continue to add to your list as more ideas come up.

Then, use this web graphic organizer to brainstorm ways to address one of these needs.

Need: _____

Unit 3

Katie Stagliano

Katie's Krops

Katie Stagliano loves growing food and feeding people. It all started when she was nine. She grew a gigantic cabbage and donated it to a local **soup kitchen**. She wanted to feed people in need.

> "I brought home this cabbage seedling as part of a school project, and planted it in our backyard, watering and weeding around it every day. Once it grew into a 40-pound cabbage, we knew it was far too big for just my family. If one cabbage can feed 275 people, imagine how many people an entire garden could feed. That was the inspiration for my **volunteerism**. I wanted to help feed people in need."[1]

Katie told teachers at her school that she wanted to start a community garden. She wanted to grow food for anyone who needed it. The school let Katie have a piece of land for her garden that was the size of a football field. With help from family and friends, Katie grew vegetables including tomatoes, peppers, cucumbers, beans, eggplant, okra, and more. Everything she grew went to feed people in need.

> "Katie's Krops has helped many, many, many people. I've grown thousands of pounds of produce to donate to people who are struggling with **food insecurity**. The food I am bringing them helps in more ways than just feeding them."[2]

Food Insecurity

Many people in America suffer from food insecurity. About one out of every nine Americans is food insecure. This means that they can't always get healthy food. Some people experience food insecurity for a little while and others for a long time.

- Food insecurity can be caused by not having enough money to buy healthy food.
- Some people who are sick or disabled can't go out and buy food.
- Some people live in places where there aren't a lot of grocery stores or farmers markets, so it is hard to get healthy food.

Katie wants kids to know they will have healthy food to eat. She believes that when you are hungry, you cannot focus on school. If kids are not hungry, they will be comfortable in class. They can focus on learning. Being able to concentrate helps build a better future for all of us.

1. Points of Light. "Crops For Change: Volunteers Grow Gardens Nationwide To Feed Hungry Families Amidst Coronavirus." Katie's Krops. May 20, 2020.
2. Points of Light. "Crops For Change: Volunteers Grow Gardens Nationwide To Feed Hungry Families Amidst Coronavirus." Katie's Krops. May 20, 2020.

Katie Stagliano (cont.)

More Gardens for More Food

Katie wanted to help even more people. She heard from kids all over the country who wanted to help, too. She received **donations** from others who wanted to help. She was able to give **grants** to kids to start their own gardens. They could use the money to buy plants, tools, and whatever else they need to get started.

Katie's Krops grew to over 100 gardens in 30 states in eight years. Kids run gardens in their backyards, in schoolyards, and anywhere they can get permission to grow. They donate their harvests to help feed people suffering from food insecurity.

> "I believe the power of youth is something that needs to be tapped into more. … When I first began Katie's Krops, I was only nine years old and had a big dream to end hunger. I was amazed by the support I received from youth across the country and how many kids wanted to get involved. I wanted to pay it forward to other youth and help them follow their dreams. That's why I decided to give grants to other youth to help them start vegetable gardens and donate the produce to feed those in need in their community."[3]

New Challenges and New Solutions

When the COVID-19 pandemic hit, Katie knew she had to make some changes. Kids were stuck at home when school buildings closed, so they couldn't work in their school gardens. Katie started a seed **distribution** program. Kids get a letter in the mail with seed packets of cantaloupes, tomatoes, peppers, and more easy-to-grow crops. They can grow food for their own families and for neighbors. If they don't have a yard, they can grow food in pots.

The pandemic also meant people couldn't eat together in the **traditional** way at soup kitchens. How would people in need get food? Katie started a weekly program where people could pick up meals to take home. Her group focuses on making healthy meals that will keep everyone's **immune systems** healthy. They use the food they grow and add donations like pasta from different companies. People come in cars, on bikes, and on foot to pick up the healthy meals. She tries to make the meals fun and different each time, too.

3. Aschenbrand-Robinson, Rachel. "Empowered Woman Wednesday: How Katie Stagliano is Fighting Hunger in the U.S. (And How You Can Help!)" January 31, 2020.

Unit 3

Name: _____ Date: _____

Key Ideas and Details

Directions: Answer the questions below about Katie Stagliano. Use complete sentences.

1. If you were going to tell someone what this text is about, what would you say?

   _____

   _____

2. How did Katie get started growing food?

   _____

   _____

3. What happened that made Katie change the way she helped feed people?

   _____

   _____

   What did she do in this new situation?

   _____

   _____

   _____

4. What is *food insecurity*?

   _____

   _____

   _____

Name: _____ **Date:** _____

Craft and Structure

Directions: Answer the questions below. Use complete sentences.

1. What is a *grant*? Use the sentences around the word to help you understand it.

   _____
   _____
   _____
   _____
   _____
   _____

2. Why do you think the author included quotes from Katie Stagliano?

   _____
   _____
   _____
   _____
   _____
   _____

3. How does the sidebar about food insecurity help you understand the rest of the text?

   _____
   _____
   _____
   _____
   _____
   _____

Unit 3

Name: _____ Date: _____

Integration of Knowledge and Meaning

Directions: Answer the questions below. Use complete sentences.

1. The author starts by stating, "Katie Stagliano loves growing food and feeding people." What details in the text support this statement?

   _____
   _____
   _____
   _____
   _____
   _____

2. Katie wants to help people get healthy food to eat. How can this help kids in school? How do you know?

   _____
   _____
   _____
   _____
   _____
   _____

3. What other ways do you think having access to healthy food helps people?

   _____
   _____
   _____
   _____
   _____
   _____

Name: _____ Date: _____

Group Discussion

Brainstorming: Katie's family couldn't eat all of the 40-pound cabbage she grew, so they decided to share it with others in their community. Maybe you have clothes you have outgrown or toys you don't play with anymore. Or, maybe you have extra time to spend helping others. What else might you have more of than you need? How could you share it with others in your community?

―――――― **Taking Action** ――――――

Directions: Think of something you could share with others in your community. It could be material things, time, or your skills or talents. Fill out the graphic organizer to plan your sharing.

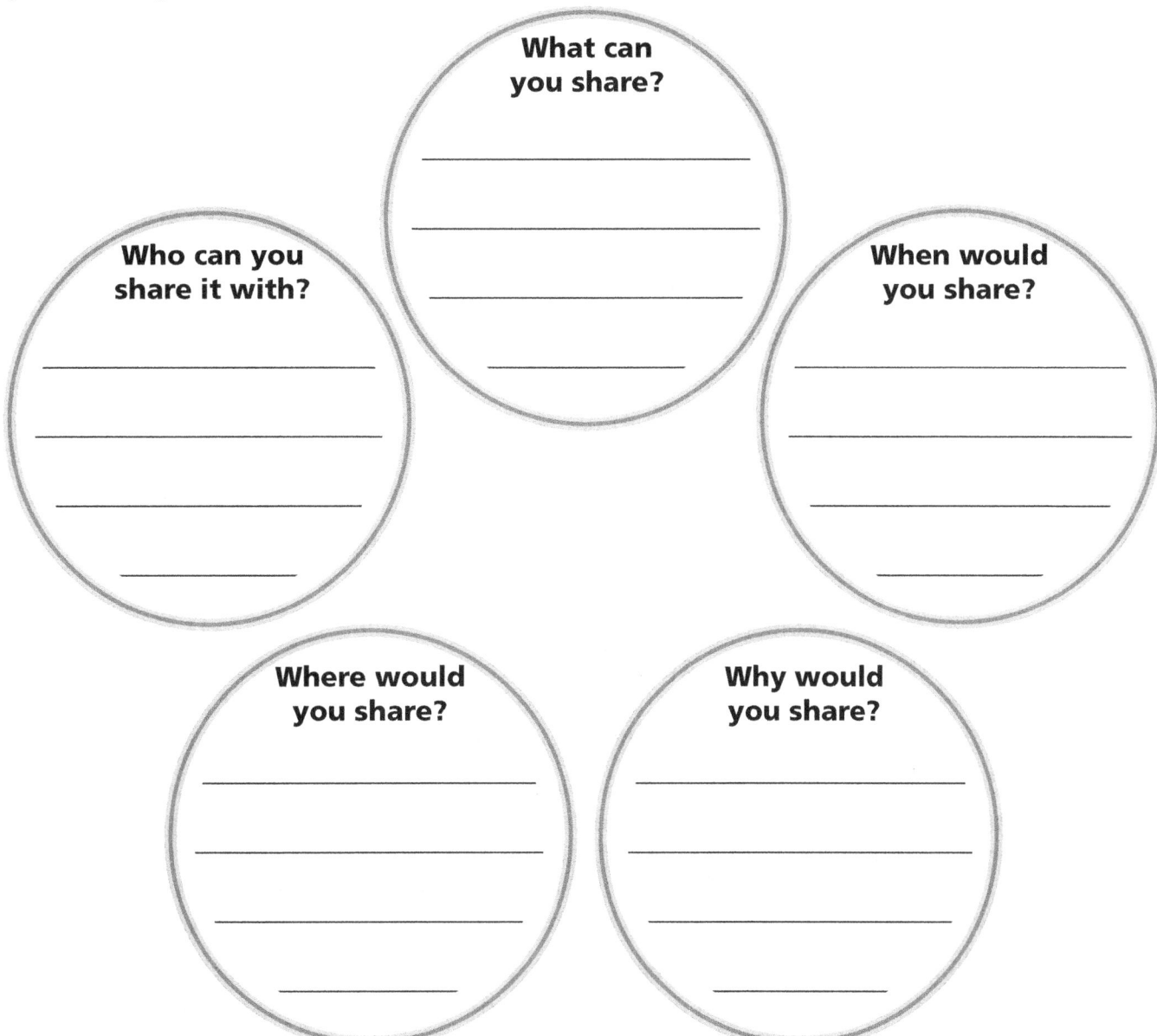

Unit 4

Shanneil Turner

Basketball Dreams

Shanneil Turner loves basketball. As a young player, she practiced all the time and planned to try out for her high school team. But she didn't have a good pair of athletic shoes. The old shoes she had borrowed were ripped, and her family could not afford to buy her a new pair. How could she play her best with a pair of sneakers held together by duct tape?

Shanneil had been a member of her local Boys and Girls Club since she was six. The Boys and Girls Club is a neighborhood place kids can go after school for homework help, sports, and other activities. Shanneil's club gave her a **scholarship** to buy basketball shoes. With the right footwear, Shanneil's tryout went well. Her years of hard work paid off, and she made the high school basketball team. Shanneil knew that if it hadn't been for the scholarship, she probably wouldn't have been able to play. She thought that other kids might be in the same **predicament**. She didn't want a pair of shoes to stand in the way of a kid's sports dreams.

➡ **predicament**—a difficult, unpleasant, or embarrassing situation

Shanneil's Locker

> "There are some kids out there who won't even try because they know they don't have what they need."[1]

Shanneil went to the Boys and Girls Club. She told them she wanted to raise money to help more kids get the sports equipment they need to play. She wanted to pay it forward. The Boys and Girls Club liked her idea. They decided to call the program Shanneil's Locker. Shanneil was 15 when the program began.

A local newspaper ran a story about Shanneil's Locker. An **executive** at a large company read the story and was impressed by what Shanneil was trying to do. She contacted Shanneil and told her about a **grant** from her company to help promote exercise and healthy lifestyles. She helped Shanneil apply. Shanneil's Locker was awarded a grant.

A state assemblyman also saw the newspaper story. He was impressed to see a 15-year-old working to help others. He donated money to Shanneil's Locker. He also awarded her a Certificate of Appreciation from the state assembly.

1. Hicks, Bill. "Shanneil's Locker opens door for youth sports," Daily Republic, February 7, 2016.

Shanneil Turner (cont.)

Shanneil's Locker (cont.)

The Boys and Girls Club held a big event to **launch** Shanneil's Locker. Kids at the event got Shanneil's Locker T-shirts signed by Shanneil. They helped give out scholarship applications to other kids. People were asked to donate to support the program.

> ➡ **launch**—start; introduce; open

Altogether, Shanneil raised enough money to give scholarships to 100 kids. The application for Shanneil's Locker scholarships asks what sport the applicant plans to play. It also asks how they plan to "pay it forward."

Each recipient gets a **voucher** they can use to buy athletic shoes from one of two shoe companies. The companies are helping by offering extra discounts to the Shanneil's Locker scholarship recipients.

Pay It Forward

Have you ever heard the saying, "pay it forward"? It means that when someone does something nice for you, instead of paying them back, you do something nice for another person. Imagine that you hold a door open for someone. That person might pay it forward by holding a door for someone else, offering their seat on the bus to someone who looks tired, or helping a neighbor with some chores. The chain of good deeds keeps going.

When Shanneil received a scholarship from the Boys and Girls Club, she wanted to pay it forward. So she started Shanneil's Locker to help other kids.

Recipients of her scholarships are also asked to pay it forward and keep the kindness going.

Unit 4

Name: _____ Date: _____

Key Ideas and Details

Directions: Answer the questions below about Shanneil Turner. Use complete sentences.

1. What is the main idea of this text?

   _____
   _____
   _____
   _____

2. Why did Shanneil want to help kids get new athletic shoes?

   _____
   _____
   _____
   _____

3. How did people find out about Shanneil's Locker?

   _____
   _____
   _____
   _____

4. What does the application for Shanneil's Locker scholarships ask?

   _____
   _____
   _____
   _____

Name: _____   Date: _____

Craft and Structure

Directions: Answer the questions below. Use complete sentences.

1. What is a *voucher*?

   _____
   _____
   _____

2. Why do you think the author chose to include a sidebar on the expression "pay it forward"?

   _____
   _____
   _____
   _____

3. Choose one word from the text that you think is important to understanding Shanneil's story. Define the word and explain its importance to the story.

   Word: _____

   Definition: _____

   Importance to the story: _____
   _____
   _____
   _____
   _____
   _____

Unit 4

Name: _____ Date: _____

Integration of Knowledge and Meaning

Directions: Answer the questions below. Use complete sentences.

1. How did Shanneil get money for her project?

   _____
   _____
   _____

   What else might she have done to raise money?

   _____
   _____
   _____

2. Why does Shanneil's Locker ask kids to pay it forward?

   _____
   _____
   _____
   _____

3. What are some examples of things kids could do to pay it forward?

   _____
   _____
   _____
   _____

Name: _____   Date: _____

Unit 4

Group Discussion

Brainstorming: Have you ever paid it forward? What did someone do for you? What did you do to pay it forward? If you haven't had an opportunity to pay it forward yet, what would you do if you did?

Taking Action

Paying it forward creates a ripple of kindness.

Directions: Think of ways to spread a message in your community to remind people to pay it forward.

What is your message?

_____
_____
_____
_____
_____

How will you spread your message in your community?

_____
_____
_____
_____
_____

Unit 5

Sidney Keys III

Seeing Himself in Stories

Sidney Keys III likes swimming, soccer, basketball, video games, and photography. But his favorite thing is reading. When Sidney was young, he had a stutter. Other kids teased him. Sidney found that reading helped him escape into a good story. He liked that he could see the story in his mind and play out all the events.

But Sidney had a problem with the books he was reading. He didn't see many characters that looked like him.

> "**Fantasy** is something that I really like a lot. Growing up as a kid I always wanted to be…a knight or to be…a king…. But every knight and king that I saw did not look like me at all. But, if I were able to see characters that look like me, it would have been a lot easier for me to say, hey, I'm a king, too. I'm a Black king."[1]

Sidney started seeking out books with African American characters. His mom took him to a special bookshop. They had many books with African American characters. He sat on the floor of the shop and read book after book. Sidney loved seeing himself in stories.

Sidney asked if there was a book club at the store. They said it was only for girls. So Sidney decided to start a new book club for boys.

Sharing the Joy of Reading

Sidney wanted to share books with other boys. He wanted to show them how awesome reading could be. He loved getting lost in a good book and letting his imagination soar, especially when he could see himself in the characters. So at 10 years old, Sidney started his book club. He started with just seven boys, ages 7 to 12. They met to discuss books and to make friends. He called it Books N Bros.

Sidney loved Books N Bros. He enjoyed talking about books and sharing ideas with different kids his age. It was fun. He wanted more boys to share his experience and discover stories and African American characters they could relate to.

He worked with his mom to grow his book club idea. They expanded the age range to include more members. They started a website to help people form their own Books N Bros clubs. Some **publishers** donated books for kids who couldn't afford them. Companies donated money. The idea grew and grew. Books N Bros now has over 400 members in the United States and Canada. Sidney chooses a book each month that features African American stories. All of the Books N Bros members read the story, and groups meet once a month to talk about it.

1. Cartoon Network. "Drawn to Making It Happen | Black History Month | Cartoon Network." YouTube, February 6, 2021.

Sidney Keys III (cont.)

A Specific Problem

Why does Books N Bros only include boys? Research shows that many boys between the ages of 8 and 12 stop reading for pleasure. Because the best way to get good at reading is to read a lot, boys often fall behind girls in school. Books N Bros wants boys to experience the power and the joy of reading. The book clubs feature different types of books each month. This keeps it interesting and helps boys improve their reading skills.

Books N Bros members do not have to be Black. All boys who want to read African American stories are welcome! Some members didn't even like to read when they started. Usually, a family member had signed them up! Sidney finds that, often, these boys end up having fun at the group meetings and start to read the books in order to talk about the books, too.

Mirrors and Windows

Stories in books, movies, TV shows, and other media can be "mirrors" and "windows."

 Stories can be mirrors when kids see themselves and people like them as characters. It helps them feel that they matter in the world.

 Stories can be windows when kids see characters that are different from them. Story windows help students in many ways. They can

- learn more about their world.
- break down **stereotypes** they may have formed.
- develop **empathy** for others.

⇒ **stereotype**—to believe unfairly that all people or things with a particular characteristic are the same	⇒ **empathy**—the ability to imagine and understand the feelings of others; the act of being aware and understanding the feelings and thoughts of another person or group

Exploring New Books

It is important to find stories about characters that you have things in common with. It is also important to read about people who are different from you. Seek out stories about people with different abilities and different likes and dislikes. Look for characters that wear different clothes and hairstyles, celebrate different holidays, and live in different places with different kinds of families.

Unit 5

Name: _____ **Date:** _____

Key Ideas and Details

Directions: Answer the questions below about Sidney Keys III. Use complete sentences.

1. Who is this text about? What are two things the text tells you about him?

   _____
   _____
   _____
   _____

2. What problem did Sidney have with the books he was reading?

   _____
   _____
   _____
   _____

3. Why did Sidney start the Books N Bros book club? How do you know?

   _____
   _____
   _____
   _____

4. How did the book club grow from seven boys to over 400?

   _____
   _____
   _____
   _____

Unit 5

Name: _____   Date: _____

Craft and Structure

Directions: Answer the questions below. Use complete sentences.

1. Why do you think the author included the section with the subhead, "A Specific Problem"?

   _____
   _____
   _____
   _____
   _____

2. Why do you think the author chose to put the information about "Mirrors and Windows" in an inset?

   _____
   _____
   _____
   _____
   _____

3. What does the word *empathy* mean? How does it relate to reading books?

   _____
   _____
   _____
   _____
   _____
   _____

©Teacher Created Resources   #9105 Kids Taking Action

Unit 5

Name: _____ Date: _____

Integration of Knowledge and Meaning

Directions: Answer the questions below. Use complete sentences.

1. What reasons does the text state for why Books N Bros only includes boys? Do you think this is a good idea? Why, or why not?

   _____
   _____
   _____
   _____
   _____
   _____

2. What are your favorite "mirror" stories?

   _____
   _____
   _____
   _____
   _____
   _____

3. What are your favorite "window" stories?

   _____
   _____
   _____
   _____
   _____
   _____
   _____

Name: _____   Date: _____

Unit 5

Group Discussion

Brainstorming: Have you ever been in a club? Why did you join? Why do people join clubs or groups? What are the advantages and disadvantages of clubs and groups?

Taking Action

Sidney Keys III had a specific problem he wanted to solve: he didn't see characters in books that looked like him. He found that others had the same problem, and so he started a book club to help solve it.

What is a specific problem that you have that others might have as well?

_____

_____

_____

How could you find out if others have the same problem?

_____

_____

_____

What kind of group could you create to help yourself and others address the problem?

_____

_____

_____

©Teacher Created Resources #9105 Kids Taking Action

Unit 6

Lesein Mutunkei

Lesein's Two Loves

Lesein Mutunkei grew up loving the outdoors. His family spent weekends and holidays visiting parks around their hometown of Nairobi, Kenya. They went camping and hiking. They participated in charity walks and sometimes planted trees. They knew that **deforestation** was a threat to the environment, and they wanted to help make a difference.

Lesein also loves sports. He plays tennis, runs, and swims. He has a lot of energy! His favorite sport is one that is played in 200 countries across the world. It is the most popular sport. Where Lesein lives, it is called *football*; and in the United States, it is called *soccer*. He joined a club team and became one of their best scoring players. When he got to high school, he joined the school team as well.

One Little Thing

Lesein takes inspiration from Wangari Maathai, the first African woman and the first **environmentalist** to win the Nobel Peace Prize. Dr. Maathai, a science professor from Kenya, started a **grassroots** movement to fight deforestation. She saw that **native** forests were being cut down to grow crops like coffee, tea, and sugarcane.

> "Cutting down the **indigenous** forests and replacing them with **exotic** species of trees caused everything else to die." [1]

Dr. Maathai encouraged people to do "one little thing" to make a difference in the world. She believed in the power of many people combining their individual efforts to make big changes. She started the Greenbelt Movement and encouraged women to plant trees in their local environment. Her efforts led to the planting of over 30 million trees across Africa. She was **affectionately** known by people in Kenya as "Mama Trees."

> "It's the little things citizens do. That's what will make the difference. My little thing is planting trees."
> —Wangari Maathai [2]

➡ **deforestation**—the purposeful clearing of forest land by humans for other uses

1. "Lesein Mutunkei." It's Time, a Festival of Climate Action. Accessed April 25, 2021.
2. Stallard, Jackie. "Words to Live By—A Tribute to Wangari Maathai." Project Learning Tree, August 21, 2019.

Lesein Mutunkei (cont.)

So Many Trees!

When he was about 12 years old, Lesein learned more about environmental threats such as deforestation, climate change, and plastic pollution. He did some research online. He learned that about 5 million trees are cut down in Kenya every day. He wanted to visualize what that many trees looked like. Using math, he figured out that every hour Kenya loses enough trees to fill about six professional soccer fields. Lesein decided he needed to do something to help.

> "I didn't want to lose what I had, like going for nature walks or mountain climbing or camping."[3]

Trees for Goals

Lesein wanted to use his love of soccer to help plant trees. He decided to plant a tree for every goal he scored. He called his project Trees4Goals. In one year, he planted 109 trees! It made him feel good and **motivated** him to play even better.

The next year, Lesein expanded his project. Kenya's Ministry of Environment heard about Trees4Goals. They agreed to provide him with trees. Lesein planted 11 trees for every goal scored by his team, because there are 11 players on a soccer team. So far, he has planted over 1,400 trees around Nairobi.

Kids at Lesein's school became interested in his project. He showed them how to plant trees. He got other sports teams at his school to join his project. The basketball team started Hoops4Trees. He got teachers to help kids plant trees on their school field trip to a national park in Southern Kenya.

Lesein has big goals for himself and his project. He wants to create a Trees4Goals forest in every county in Kenya, and then every country in Africa. He hopes to get the international soccer organization FIFA to start planting trees. Through social media, he spreads his message to encourage other young people to help make a difference.

> "I always say: you are never too small or too young to make an impact in the world. Remember that everything you do, however small, counts."[4]

---

3. "Kenyan Football Teen Plants Trees for Goals." BBC News. BBC. Accessed April 25, 2021.
4. "Lesein Mutunkei." It's Time, a Festival of Climate Action. Accessed April 25, 2021.

Unit 6

Name: _____ Date: _____

Key Ideas and Details

Directions: Answer the questions below about Lesein Mutunkei. Use complete sentences.

1. In what country and city does Lesein Mutunkei live? On which continent does he live?

   _____
   _____
   _____
   _____

2. What problem did Lesein want to help solve?

   _____
   _____
   _____
   _____

3. How did Lesein use math to better understand *deforestation*?

   _____
   _____
   _____
   _____

4. Who was Wangari Maathai? How did she influence Lesein?

   _____
   _____
   _____
   _____

Unit 6

Name: _____ Date: _____

Craft and Structure

Directions: Answer the questions below. Use complete sentences.

1. What does it mean to be an *environmentalist*?

   _____
   _____
   _____
   _____
   _____
   _____

2. Why do you think the author included the sidebar about Dr. Maathai?

   _____
   _____
   _____
   _____
   _____
   _____
   _____

3. What is the idea that ties the parts of this text together?

   _____
   _____
   _____
   _____
   _____
   _____
   _____

Unit 6

Name: _____ Date: _____

Integration of Knowledge and Meaning

Directions: Answer the questions below. Use complete sentences.

1. How did Lesein choose to help solve the problem of deforestation?

   _____
   _____
   _____
   _____

   Why do you think he chose this course of action? How do you know?

   _____
   _____
   _____
   _____

2. Do you think Lesein's project was successful? Why, or why not?

   _____
   _____
   _____
   _____

3. What else would you like to know about Lesein Mutunkei and Trees4Goals?

   _____
   _____
   _____
   _____

Name: _____   Date: _____

Unit 6

Group Discussion

Brainstorming: Lesein uses Dr. Maathai's idea of doing "one little thing" to help make a difference in the world. What are some ideas for your one little thing? What difference could it make if many people did the same little thing?

―――― **Taking Action** ――――

Lesein planted trees to help his community. That is his "one little thing."

Directions: Think of a problem in your community and one little thing you could do to help. Complete this graphic organizer to help you come up with a plan.

What is your "one little thing" you can do?
_____
_____

⬇

How could you get others to join you?
_____
_____
_____

⬇

What effect could the efforts of many people working together have on the problem?
_____
_____
_____

©Teacher Created Resources   #9105 Kids Taking Action

Unit 7
Janine Licare and Aislin Livingstone

Growing Up in the Rainforest

Janine Licare and Aislin Livingstone grew up together in Costa Rica. They were best friends. They lived in an area surrounded by rainforest. It was a beautiful **ecosystem**.

> ➡ **ecosystem**—a home for many different types of plants and animals that depend on one another to live

Each day, Janine and Aislin walked to school through the rainforest. They loved to watch the monkeys playing in the trees. When they learned that parts of their rainforest were being cut down, they worried about what would happen to the monkeys. **Deforestation** affects animals, plants, and people. They knew that many monkeys were being hurt or killed trying to cross the busy roads or climbing on new electrical wires. How would the monkeys move from one part of the rainforest to another for food, water, or shelter if more trees were cut down?

> **Habitat fragmentation** happens when the areas where animals live are split up into sections by roads, buildings, or other structures. Then, there is no way for animals to travel safely between them. Animals can be hurt or killed trying to cross roads, train tracks, or other hazards to get to their food and water.

Getting Started

Janine and Aislin decided they needed to do something. The girls made papier-mâché bottles and painted rock paperweights. They set up a cardboard box next to a local shop and sold their artwork.

> "When your backyard is being torn apart in front of your own eyes, anyone would be compelled to try and save it."[1]

They raised $80 and got Aislin's mom to match that amount. They now had $160 to save the rainforest. They donated the money to a local organization. Sadly, when they went to visit, no one could tell them what had been done with their money. The girls were disappointed. They decided to start their own charity so they could keep track of what the money was used for.

1. Onemoregeneration. "Kids Saving the Rainforest." National Geographic Education Blog, April 13, 2016.

Janine Licare and Aislin Livingstone (cont.)

Kids Saving the Rainforest

Aislin and Janine were nine years old when they founded Kids Saving the Rainforest (KSTR). They raised money and gave it to Janine's mom who bought four **acres** of land and some **saplings** to plant on it. But the girls didn't stop there!

- They kept raising money to **reforest** the land. They started an adopt-a-tree program. Kids can have a sapling planted in their friend's name. KSTR has planted over 300 acres to keep growing **native** trees. These trees provide good habitats for rainforest animals.

- The girls also wrote "Eleven Reasons Not to Feed the Monkeys." They handed copies out to tourists in national parks. They wanted to remind people that monkeys are wild animals and should not get too close to humans or eat human food.

- KSTR builds "monkey bridges." These bridges are ropes strung from tree to tree high up in the air. Monkeys and other animals use them to travel safely above roads, power lines, and other dangers. These bridges have helped double the population of the squirrel monkey, which was once endangered.

- The girls also started a wildlife **sanctuary** to care for orphaned and injured animals. At the KSTR rescue center, animals are given medical care. When possible, the animals are released back into the wild. Animals that cannot be released are cared for at the sanctuary, where visitors can learn about them. Veterinarians, biologists, and volunteers all help care for the animals. They care for monkeys, sloths, kinkajous, coatis, parrots, and more.

Wildlife Crossings

Animals need to be able to travel to all parts of their habitats. They need food and water and to find mates. More and more trees are being cut down to make room for humans. This means smaller, divided habitats for animals.

In many places, people build wildlife crossings to help animals travel safely from one part of their habitat to another. Here are some different types of crossings:

- Bridges help rainforest animals like monkeys and sloths travel safely above power lines and roads. These can be as simple as a sturdy rope stretched between trees.

- "Turtle tunnels" help turtles in Japan safely cross underneath railroad tracks.

- Underpasses and overpasses have been built to help animals cross highways safely.

- On Christmas Island, special crab bridges and tunnels allow hundreds of millions of red crabs to safely cross roads each year.

- Salmon need to go upstream to reproduce. "Salmon cannons" and fish ladders help fish in the Pacific Northwest get over dams.

Unit 7

Name: _____ Date: _____

Key Ideas and Details

Directions: Answer the questions below about Janine Licare and Aislin Livingstone. Use complete sentences.

1. Who is this passage about? What are three details it tells you about them?

   _____
   _____
   _____
   _____

2. Why did Janine and Aislin want to save the rainforest?

   _____
   _____
   _____
   _____

3. What does Kids Saving the Rainforest do?

   _____
   _____
   _____
   _____

4. How do wildlife crossings help animals?

   _____
   _____
   _____
   _____

Name: _____ **Date:** _____

Craft and Structure

Directions: Answer the questions below. Use complete sentences.

1. What does *reforest* mean?

   _____

   _____

   _____

   _____

2. Why do you think the author chose to use bulleted lists in this text?

   _____

   _____

   _____

   _____

3. Choose one word from the text that you think is important to understanding Janine and Aislin's story. Define the word and explain its importance to the story.

   Word: _____

   Definition: _____

   _____

   Importance to the story: _____

   _____

   _____

   _____

   _____

Unit 7

Name: _____ Date: _____

Integration of Knowledge and Meaning

Directions: Answer the questions below. Use complete sentences.

1. The author states that humans are causing animal habitats to become smaller and divided. What reasons are given in the text to support this?

   _____
   _____
   _____
   _____
   _____

2. How did Janine and Aislin raise money for Kids Saving the Rainforest?

   _____
   _____
   _____

   Do you think the author gave you enough information about this? Why, or why not?

   _____
   _____
   _____

3. What more would you like to know about Kids Saving the Rainforest? Why?

   _____
   _____
   _____
   _____

Unit 7

Name: _____ Date: _____

Group Discussion

Brainstorming: What animals live in habitats near you? What problems do they face? How do you know? How could you find out more?

Taking Action

Directions: Use this graphic organizer to do research and plan a project.

What is the problem? _____
_____
_____

What is already being done? _____
_____
_____

What can I do to help? _____
_____
_____

What challenges might I face?	What kinds of help might I need?	Who might be able to help?
_____	_____	_____
_____	_____	_____
_____	_____	_____
_____	_____	_____

©Teacher Created Resources   #9105 Kids Taking Action

Unit 8
Salvador Gómez-Colón

Hurricane Maria

Fifteen-year-old Salvador Gómez-Colón looked out the window of his apartment. All he saw was destruction. Hurricane Maria had hit the island of Puerto Rico. It **devastated** much of the island. Some homes were destroyed completely. Others were heavily damaged. Many people lost everything they owned. Power was out everywhere. There was no electricity. Water supplies were cut off.

> "I felt like I had woken up to a nightmare. Outside my flooded apartment, I saw fallen branches and streetlamps, shattered windows, and homes without roofs. The parks where I played growing up and the streets I **frequented** for most of my life had disappeared."[1]

Luckier Than Most

Salvador and his family were lucky. Their apartment was still standing. They had some food and water, though they had to **ration** it. They also had a **generator** that made some electricity. The generator allowed them to charge their cell phones. It also gave them enough power to have one light on at night.

Salvador stared out the window and saw nothing but darkness. He couldn't stop thinking about all the people out there in the dark. He worried that someone would trip and fall. Emergency services would not be able to get to them because the roads were blocked.

In the daytime, Salvador saw many families who had made temporary roofs out of tarps or broken pieces of their houses. He saw kids sitting in the hot sun, rushing to finish their homework. They had no light to work after dark. He also saw that many people were still wearing the same clothes they had on when the hurricane struck. They had no way to do laundry. Salvador wanted to find a way to help.

➦ **ration**—use in small amounts; use for a short amount of time

Natural Disasters

Earthquakes, floods, hurricanes, tornados, and wildfires are all natural disasters. They can cause a lot of damage. We can't stop natural disasters from happening, but we can be prepared. It is a good idea to have an emergency kit with supplies. After a disaster, you might need water, food, first-aid supplies, flashlights, and other important items. It is important to have a plan to evacuate if you need to. You also need a plan for where to meet if you get separated.

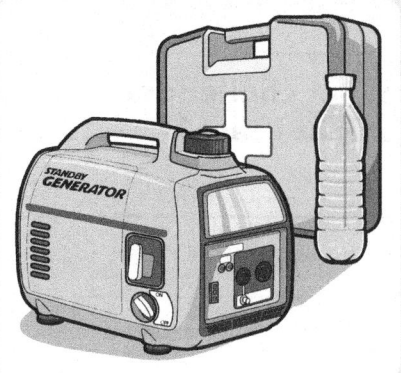

1. Gómez-Colón, Salvador. "We Need Empathy in Times of Crisis. But That Doesn't Just Mean Feeling for Others." TIME.com. May 21, 2020.

Salvador Gómez-Colón (cont.)

Luckier Than Most (cont.)

> "I couldn't bear the thought of thousands of people losing their belongings, homes, and family members. Rather than rest on the privilege of having a roof over my head and a family to turn to, I **vowed** to create a positive impact. Rather than merely speak up, I wanted to take action, concrete action."[2]

Concrete Action

Salvador used his phone to text a friend of his mother's in New York. He knew she helped provide solar-powered lamps to people in need in Africa. Salvador asked her to help him do the same for Puerto Rico. She set up an online **crowdfunding** campaign for Salvador called Light and Hope for Puerto Rico. People were able to donate money on the Light and Hope website to give solar lamps and hand-powered washing machines to people in Puerto Rico. Salvador also contacted companies that make solar lights. Some of them donated lights. They also sold some lights to him at a discount.

Results

Salvador's efforts worked! When he started receiving supplies, his family, friends, and other volunteers helped him **distribute** them. The solar lamps helped people cook and do homework. It was safer for kids and disabled people to move around at night. People could also use the solar power to charge their cell phones. The hand-crank washing machines helped people have clean clothes to wear. These things gave people hope and made their lives better.

Over several months, Salvador raised nearly $200,000. He distributed solar lamps and hand-crank washing machines to 3,500 families. Since then, he has started other projects. He helped people after Hurricane Dorian in the Bahamas. He helped after earthquakes caused more damage in Puerto Rico. Salvador shows that young people can combine empathy and action to make a difference.

> "In our moments of crisis, **empathy** doesn't mean merely feeling for others. It requires turning our emotions into positive actions, with the common purpose of supporting each other."[3]

---

2. Gómez Colón, Salvador. "My world, reimagined: When youth have a seat at the table." Voices of Youth, June 5, 2020.
3. Salvador Gómez-Colón for TIME magazine, accessed April 25, 2021.

Unit 8

Name: _____ **Date:** _____

Key Ideas and Details

Directions: Answer the questions below about Salvador Gómez-Colón. Use complete sentences.

1. If you were going to create a new title for this text, what would it be, and why?

   _____

   _____

2. What kinds of problems did people in Puerto Rico face after the hurricane?

   _____

   _____

   _____

3. How did Salvador get help for people?

   _____

   _____

   _____

   _____

4. What is a *natural disaster*? What examples are given in the text?

   _____

   _____

   _____

   _____

Name: _____ **Date:** _____

Craft and Structure

Directions: Answer the questions below. Use complete sentences.

1. What is *crowdfunding*? Use context clues to help you understand it.

   _____
   _____
   _____
   _____
   _____

2. What is the idea that ties all the parts of this text together?

   _____
   _____
   _____
   _____
   _____

3. In the first quote, Salvador gives a first-person account of what he saw after the hurricane. Why do you think the author included this quote in addition to writing about the damage?

   _____
   _____
   _____
   _____
   _____

Unit 8

Name: _____   Date: _____

Integration of Knowledge and Meaning

Directions: Answer the questions below. Use complete sentences.

1. The author writes, "Salvador and his family were lucky." What details in the text support this statement?

   _____
   _____
   _____
   _____
   _____

2. How can solar-powered lamps be helpful to people after a natural disaster? How do you know?

   _____
   _____
   _____
   _____
   _____

3. What other supplies might be helpful to people after a natural disaster? How might they help?

   _____
   _____
   _____
   _____
   _____

Unit 8

Name: _____ Date: _____

Group Discussion

Brainstorming: What is *empathy*? How do we understand the feelings of others? Talk about a time when you empathized with someone. How did you know what they were feeling? Did you do anything about it? Why, or why not?

Taking Action

Salvador knows that empathy—the ability to share the feelings of others—is important. But he believes that empathy alone is not enough. We can use empathy as a starting point for action.

Directions: Choose a problem that your community faces. Either interview someone who faces this problem or list what you think the responses would be. Use the Empathy Map below to record evidence about how they feel. Then, use this information to clarify the problem and make a plan of action.

Problem: _____

Who has this problem? _____

What did they say?	What did they do?
Empathy Map	
What did they think?	What did they feel?

What did you learn about how people are experiencing the problem? _____
_____

What did you learn about what people need? _____
_____

What can you do to help? _____
_____

©Teacher Created Resources   #9105 Kids Taking Action

Unit 9

Areeta Wong

Hooked on Coding

Areeta Wong learned about computer **coding** through a summer program. She got to spend two weeks learning about how computers are used at a big company. Areeta loved computer coding. She was hooked!

Areeta took all the computer classes she could at her high school. She became a teacher's assistant for her school's Introduction to Computer Science class. She became president of her local Girls Who Code club. She also went to her first **hackathon**.

> ⇒ **coding**—writing script in a language that a computer can understand

When Areeta attended the hackathon, she just didn't feel like she fit in. Most of the attendees were boys. So Areeta decided to start her own hackathon to introduce more girls to coding.

"For every fifteen guys at a hackathon, there are only two girls. I've started Superposition, which is a hackathon aimed at high school girls … of all experience levels and backgrounds. My team wants to offer attendees a safe, welcoming, and supportive environment to experiment with technology at any experience level."[1]

Hackathons

A hackathon is an event where people use technology to solve a problem. They **collaborate** on projects. They work together and get to know one another. Participants might create a mobile app for phones, a computer game, or a robot. A hackathon can last a few hours or a few days. Teams enjoy meals together and sometimes they work all night.

At the end, teams share their creations with one another and with the public. Sometimes, they are judged and prizes are given. Each hackathon has its own focus:

- Some are put on by companies to create new products.
- Some focus on a specific programming language or technology.
- Others want teams to create something that will help people. Teams might create an app to help stop **cyberbullying** or a website to help people find help for mental-health issues.

> ⇒ **cyberbullying**—the use of electronic communication for bullying

1. ReigningIt. "Women Who Reign: Areeta Wong," Medium, May 22, 2017.

Areeta Wong (cont.)

Superposition

Areeta's Superposition hackathon is for girls of all skill levels. Most of the girls are first-time **hackers**, and many are first-time coders. No experience is required. Areeta's team designed the event to make all feel welcome. They want girls to feel comfortable experimenting with technology and learning what it can do. They hope this will help more girls develop an interest in computer science.

> **hacker**—a person who can program and solve problems with a computer

During the hackathon, girls can take **workshops** to learn new skills. They work in teams to create new software, apps, or games. **Mentors** are available to help at any time. Free food is provided, and attendees bring sleeping bags to spend the night.

At the end of the Superposition hackathons, teams share what they have created. Judges decide which teams win prizes. Here are some winning ideas from past events:

- an app that helps identify news as real or fake
- an app for the visually impaired that describes the user's surroundings and reads street signs
- **wearables** that track and display a user's moods and display whether they'd like to be comforted or left alone

> "During the event, I saw so many smiles as they were so eager to build a project with their newfound skills and it was then where I knew I wanted to help even more students learn computer science."[2]

Branching Out

Areeta and her team loved seeing girls enjoying their hackathons. They wanted to reach out to more girls and help them learn about technology. They created a website. They helped girls build Superposition groups wherever they live. There are now 78 Superposition **chapters** in 11 countries.

Each chapter holds its own events. Their goal is to help girls feel comfortable with technology. They want to help them learn about careers in technology. Some have held workshops for girls to:

- learn new computer skills
- meet women who work in technology
- find out how to apply for **internships**
- learn how to start their own businesses

---

2. "Our Story." Superposition. Accessed April 25, 2021.

Unit 9

Name: _____   Date: _____

Key Ideas and Details

Directions: Answer the questions below about Areeta Wong. Use complete sentences.

1. What is the main idea of this text?

   _____
   _____
   _____
   _____

2. What details most helped you understand the main idea?

   _____
   _____
   _____
   _____

3. What is a *hackathon*?

   _____
   _____
   _____

4. What is the focus of Areeta's Superposition hackathon? What text evidence supports your answer?

   _____
   _____
   _____
   _____

Unit 9

Name: _____   Date: _____

Craft and Structure

Directions: Answer the questions below. Use complete sentences.

1. What does *collaborate* mean? What context clues help you understand it?

   _____

   _____

   _____

   _____

   _____

2. Why do you think the author included the sidebar on hackathons?

   _____

   _____

   _____

   _____

   _____

3. What does the writer mean by the phrase, "She was hooked" in the first paragraph?

   _____

   _____

   _____

   _____

   _____

Unit 9

Name: _____ Date: _____

Integration of Knowledge and Meaning

Directions: Answer the questions below. Use complete sentences.

1. Why do you think Areeta felt like she didn't fit in at her first hackathon?

   _____
   _____
   _____
   _____

2. Why did Areeta create a hackathon for girls?

   _____
   _____
   _____
   _____

   Do you think this is a good idea? Why, or why not?

   _____
   _____
   _____
   _____

3. What kind of hackathon would you like to participate in? Why?

   _____
   _____
   _____
   _____

Unit 9

Name: _____   Date: _____

Group Discussion

Brainstorming: Have you ever felt like you didn't fit in? Why do you think you felt that way? How can you tell if someone doesn't feel welcome in a group? What could you do to help them feel more comfortable?

Taking Action

What is a situation in which someone might not feel welcome?

Directions: Make a plan to help someone feel welcome.

Things I can say	**Things I should NOT say**

Things I can do	**Things I should NOT do**

©Teacher Created Resources

Unit 10

Jaylen Arnold

Alphabet Kid

Jaylen Arnold might seem different from most kids. He says he is differently abled. At two years old, the doctor told Jaylen's parents that he has Tourette Syndrome. When he was four years old, he was **diagnosed** with Obsessive-Compulsive Disorder. And at eight, they were told he has Asperger's Syndrome. Jaylen calls himself an "alphabet kid." This is because there are letters that describe the ways his brain controls his body and mind: Jaylen Arnold, TS, OCD, ASP. All of these cause Jaylen's body and mind to do things that other kids' don't.

> **diagnose**—observe symptoms to decide what is causing a problem and what can be done to help

- **TS:** Tourette Syndrome is when the brain causes the body to move without the person meaning it to. People with Tourette have **tics**, which are repeated movements or vocal sounds.

- **OCD:** Obsessive-Compulsive Disorder is when people have recurring, unwanted thoughts that they can't control. Some people with OCD do things over and over, like washing their hands or arranging things in a certain way.

- **ASP:** Asperger's Syndrome can make it hard for people to relate to others and make friends. They can become very interested in a topic and talk about it all the time.

Bullied

At first, Jaylen attended a small school where all the kids understood him. His classmates liked him and accepted his differences. When he was eight years old, Jaylen moved to a larger school. The kids there didn't understand why he acted differently than they did. They were not used to his behaviors. They made fun of him. He was **bullied**. Bullying is being mean to someone over and over again. Bullies use their power to hurt other people. Bullying can look like:

- teasing and calling names
- saying mean things about someone when they are not around
- leaving someone out or telling other kids not to be friends with them
- threatening to hurt someone
- forcing someone to do something they don't want to do
- hurting someone physically

Because kids were bullying him, Jaylen tried to stop his tics. Tics are kind of like sneezes. You can't hold them in forever. Trying to stop ticcing only made Jaylen's tics come back stronger. It got so bad that the tics made him hurt himself. Jaylen returned to his old school. The kids there didn't tease or bully him. He started to feel better.

Jaylen Arnold (cont.)

Bullying No Way!

When Jaylen was bullied, he didn't know what to do about it. He decided that he wanted to help other kids who are bullied. His idea was to teach kids about bullying and how to stop it. He learned about how to stop bullying. He went to schools and gave talks to the kids. He told them his story. He spread his message: "Bullying No Way!"

> "Once kids are educated about it, they won't bully so much. I put it to the test with the class at the school…where my bullying happened. It was a huge success! You should have seen all the kids coming up to me that use to make fun and copy me. They were actually telling me they were sorry! The same boys that I was scared of!"[1]

With the help of a few adults, he created "Jaylens Challenge" to help spread his anti-bullying message. Jaylens Challenge helps people learn about bullying and how to **prevent** it. It helps people **appreciate** differences in others. Jaylen got adults to help by making a website where people can learn about Jaylens Challenge. The website offers books and **workshops** that teach students, parents, and teachers how to prevent and stop bullying. Jaylens Challenge also helps kids find out how to get help if they are bullied. People can watch videos of Jaylen talking about his experiences. They can get books, wristbands, and posters to spread Jaylen's message.

Jaylen turned something bad that happened to him into something good. He has been on TV talking about his challenge. He has been honored all over the world. Jaylens Challenge has helped thousands of kids.

---

1. "Our Story: Jaylens Challenge." Our Story | Jaylens Challenge. Accessed April 25, 2021.

Unit 10

Name: _____ **Date:** _____

Key Ideas and Details

Directions: Answer the questions below about Jaylen Arnold. Use complete sentences.

1. What is this passage about?

   _____
   _____
   _____
   _____

2. What is one piece of text evidence that tells you about how Jaylen feels?

   _____
   _____
   _____
   _____

3. Why did Jaylen want to help others? How do you know?

   _____
   _____
   _____
   _____

4. What did Jaylen do to help stop bullying?

   _____
   _____
   _____
   _____

Name: _____ Date: _____

Craft and Structure

Directions: Answer the questions below. Use complete sentences.

1. What does the word *diagnosed* mean?

   _____

   _____

   _____

2. Why do you think the author chose to put the explanations of Jaylen's differences in a sidebar?

   _____

   _____

   _____

   How did the sidebar help you understand the text?

   _____

   _____

3. Why do you think the author included the quote from Jaylen?

   _____

   _____

   _____

   What does the quote tell you about Jaylen?

   _____

   _____

   _____

Unit 10

Name: _____ Date: _____

Integration of Knowledge and Meaning

Directions: Answer the questions below. Use complete sentences.

1. Do you think the author included enough information to help you understand what Jaylen went through when he was bullied?

   _____
   _____

   What else would you like to know?

   _____
   _____
   _____
   _____

2. How did Jaylen choose to combat bullying?

   _____
   _____
   _____

   Do you think he had good ideas? What else can you think of that might help?

   _____
   _____
   _____

3. Does Jaylen only want to help kids who are bullied? Who else does Jaylen's Challenge help? How do you know?

   _____
   _____
   _____
   _____

Unit 10

Name: _____   Date: _____

Group Discussion

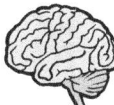 **Brainstorming:** Jaylen educates people about how to stop and prevent bullying. Have you seen or experienced bullying in your school community? What is being done already? What more could you do?

Taking Action

Jaylen used a bad experience in his life to do something positive. What bad experience in your life (or the life of someone close to you) could you turn into something positive?

Directions: Use this graphic organizer to explore your experience and how you could make a difference.

What happened?	**How did you feel?**
_____	_____
_____	_____
_____	_____
_____	_____

Experience
_____
_____

What needs to happen to change it?	**What could you do?**
_____	_____
_____	_____
_____	_____
_____	_____

©Teacher Created Resources

Unit 11

Jordan Reeves

Purple Unicorn Horn

Jordan looked around at the crowd and then down at her bright purple unicorn horn. She lifted her arm, squeezed the trigger, and whoosh! Glitter flew everywhere. She smiled. The **prosthetic** arm she designed really worked! Jordan loved it, and so did everyone else. She realized that people were seeing a disability as a positive thing.

Jordan was born with a limb difference. Her left arm stopped growing just above the elbow. Having one hand doesn't slow Jordan down! She runs, dances, plays baseball and basketball, and swims. She plays piano and trumpet. She even designed herself a 3D-printed arm so she can do push-ups!

> "If (someone is) staring, I'll say 'Don't stare, just ask.' I actually have a shirt that says that," Jordan explained. "I want them to come up and ask me. I want them to know that it's OK. It's not a bad thing. We all find our own way to do stuff."[1]

Helping Others Through Design

Each year, more than 2,000 kids with limb differences are born in the United States. Jordan wants to help other kids with limb differences. One way she helps is by making sure these kids see themselves reflected in the world around them. Jordan thinks that kids with limb differences should have dolls that look like them. She worked with a toy company to design a doll with a prosthetic leg. Now, Jordan and a group of teens work with companies to make sure that kids with disabilities are represented during the process of creating new products. She knows that this will also change the way people see disability.

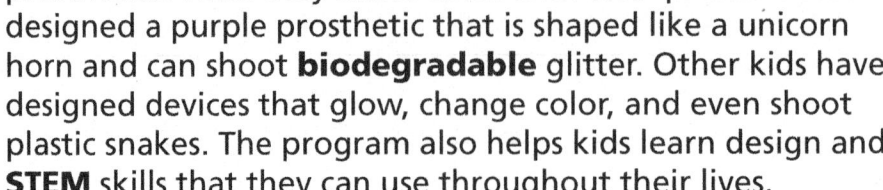

The other way Jordan is helping is by getting kids with limb differences involved in the design process. She and her mom started a project to connect kids with designers and engineers. They work together to design the kids' fun and practical ideas for prosthetics. Then they make them with a 3D printer. Jordan designed a purple prosthetic that is shaped like a unicorn horn and can shoot **biodegradable** glitter. Other kids have designed devices that glow, change color, and even shoot plastic snakes. The program also helps kids learn design and **STEM** skills that they can use throughout their lives.

➡ **biodegradable**—able to be broken down by living things

1. Krasavage, Nicole. "A Girl and Her Glitter-Shooting Prosthetic: 'You Can Do Anything.'" CNN. Cable News Network, February 13, 2017.

Jordan Reeves (cont.)

Inclusive Design

Everyone is different in their own way. Some people have differences that can make everyday things like school, work, and travel difficult. One in five Americans have some form of disability. Most people will, at some time in their lives, have a disability or know someone who has one. Some disabilities are temporary, like a broken leg. Other disabilities last throughout a person's life.

> "Our world isn't as accessible as it needs to be, so I started Born Just Right, a nonprofit that gives kids the opportunity to design. The mission is to have more accessibility in the world. My end goal is for everybody to be treated like it's not a weird thing to have a difference."[2]

Inclusive design isn't just for people with disabilities. It can make life better for everyone.

Inclusive design means making sure that people with disabilities can do things with the same amount of effort as someone who does not have a disability. It helps people be independent and live their lives without the world around them getting in their way. People of all types should be included in the design process, so that the resulting products and services are useful to everyone.

- Did you know that the idea of *text messaging* was originally designed for people who are **deaf**? The idea was expanded, and now everybody texts.

- *Automatic doors* make it possible for people who use wheelchairs or other mobility aids to go in and out of buildings easily. *Electric toothbrushes* were originally designed for people with limited mobility. Both of these inclusive designs are useful to all people.

- **Captions** make videos accessible to deaf people and those who are hard of hearing, have learning disabilities, or speak a different language. *Captions* also help everyone when they can't turn on sound or it is hard to hear or understand a video.

---

2. "Glitter Blasting Prosthetic Arm Empowers Kids with Disabilities." YouTube, July 24, 2019.

Unit 11

Name: _____ **Date:** _____

Key Ideas and Details

Directions: Answer the questions below about Jordan Reeves. Use complete sentences.

1. Who or what is this text mainly about? Think of a new title for this text.

   _____

   _____

2. How does Jordan Reeves help others?

   _____

   _____

   _____

   _____

3. What is *inclusive design*?

   _____

   _____

   _____

   _____

4. Be the teacher! What questions would a teacher ask about this text?

   _____

   _____

   _____

   _____

Name: _____   Date: _____

Unit 11

Craft and Structure

Directions: Answer the questions below. Use complete sentences.

1. What is a *prosthetic*? Use the details in the text to help you understand it.

   _____
   _____
   _____
   _____
   _____

2. Why do you think the author began the text with the story of Jordan shooting glitter?

   _____
   _____
   _____
   _____
   _____

3. How does the sidebar about inclusive design help you understand the rest of the text?

   _____
   _____
   _____
   _____
   _____
   _____

Unit 11

Name: _____ Date: _____

Integration of Knowledge and Meaning

Directions: Answer the questions below. Use complete sentences.

1. How are the sections about Jordan Reeves connected to the sidebar about inclusive design?

   _____
   _____
   _____
   _____
   _____

2. The author writes, "One way she helps is by making sure these kids see themselves reflected in the world around them. She knows that this will also change the way people see disability." How could representations of people with disabilities help change the way people see disability?

   _____
   _____
   _____
   _____
   _____

3. What does Jordan mean when she says, "We should all see disability as an opportunity."?

   _____
   _____
   _____
   _____
   _____

Name: _____   Date: _____

Unit 11

Group Discussion

Brainstorming: What does the word *inclusive* mean to you? Where and when do you feel included? In what situations might you not feel that way? When and where might others not feel included? How could your communities become more inclusive?

Taking Action

Directions: Plan to help your community become more inclusive. First, choose a community and write a short description of it in the first box. Think about the thoughts, words, and actions that people in that community might use that either exclude others or include others. Record your ideas in the chart below.

Community	

	Exclusion	Inclusion
Thoughts		
Words		
Actions		

Who might be excluded in your community?

_____

_____

How might you help the community become more inclusive?

_____

_____

©Teacher Created Resources   #9105 Kids Taking Action

Motto Bookmarks

Kids Taking Action — "Pay It Forward" —From the story about Shanneil Turner

Kids Taking Action — "If I can make a difference, you can, too." —Ryan Hickman

Kids Taking Action — "...You are never too small or too young to make an impact in the world." —Lesein Mutunkei

Kids Taking Action — "I believe in the power of youth." —Katie Stagliano

Kids Taking Action — "It's really easy to make a difference..." —Ryan Hickman

Bibliography

Unit 1: Ryan Hickman

Capo Dispatch. "Recycling Advocate Ryan Hickman, 11, Finalist for 'TIME's' Kid of the Year Award." *The Capistrano Dispatch*, November 25, 2020. https://www.thecapistranodispatch.com/recycling-advocate-ryan-hickman-11-finalist-for-times-kid-of-the-year-award/.

Unit 2: Jayera Griffin

Mason, Heather. "14-year-old Jayera Griffin is Working with Clorox to Provide Free Laundry Days to Her Community," June 22, 2018. https://amysmartgirls.com/14-year-old-jayera-griffin-is-working-with-clorox-to-provide-free-laundry-days-to-her-community-512c901b10e4.

Unit 3: Katie Stagliano

Aschenbrand-Robinson, Rachel. "Empowered Woman Wednesday: How Katie Stagliano is Fighting Hunger in the U.S. (And How You Can Help!)" Katie's Krops. January 31, 2020. https://katieskrops.com/empowered-woman-wednesday-how-katie-stagliano-is-fighting-hunger-in-the-u-s-and-how-you-can-help/.

Points of Light. "Crops For Change: Volunteers Grow Gardens Nationwide To Feed Hungry Families Amidst Coronavirus." Katie's Krops. May 20, 2020. https://katieskrops.com/crops-for-change-volunteers-grow-gardens-nationwide-to-feed-hungry-families-amidst-coronavirus/.

Unit 4: Shanneil Turner

Hicks, Bill. "Shanneil's Locker opens door for youth sports." Daily Republic, February 7, 2016. https://www.dailyrepublic.com/all-dr-news/solano-news/vacaville/question-shanneils-locker-opens-door-for-youth-sports/.

Unit 5: Sidney Keys III

Cartoon Network. "Drawn to Making It Happen | Black History Month | Cartoon Network." YouTube, February 6, 2021. https://www.youtube.com/watch?v=Pi-uxNPTL1Y.

Unit 6: Lesein Mutunkei

"Kenyan Football Teen Plants Trees for Goals." BBC News. BBC. 25 October, 2018. https://www.bbc.com/news/av/world-africa-45876475.

"Lesein Mutunkei." It's Time, a Festival of Climate Action. Accessed April 25, 2021. https://itstime.earth/speakers/lesein-mutunkei.

Stallard, Jackie. "Words to Live By—A Tribute to Wangari Maathai." Project Learning Tree, August 21, 2019. https://www.plt.org/educator-tips/words-to-live-by-tribute-wangari-maathai/.

Bibliography (cont.)

Unit 7: Janine Licare and Aislin Livingstone

Onemoregeneration. "Kids Saving The Rainforest." National Geographic Education Blog, April 13, 2016. https://blog.education.nationalgeographic.org/2016/04/13/kids-saving-the-rainforest/.

Ries, Olivia. 2016, May 18. "Monkey Bridges for Everyone" blog.education.https://blog.education.nationalgeographic.org/2016/05/18/monkey-bridges-for-everyone/.

Unit 8: Salvador Gómez-Colón

Gómez-Colón, Salvador. "We Need Empathy in Times of Crisis. But That Doesn't Just Mean Feeling for Others." TIME.com. May 21, 2020. https://time.com/5840164/empathy-coronavirus/.

Gómez Colón, Salvador. "My world, reimagined: When youth have a seat at the table." Voices of Youth, June 5, 2020. https://www.voicesofyouth.org/blog/my-world-reimagined-when-youth-have-seat-table/.

Salvador Gómez-Colón for TIME magazine, accessed April 25, 2021. https://salvadorgomezcolon.com.

Unit 9: Areeta Wong

"Our Story." Superposition. Accessed April 25, 2021. https://superposition.tech/story.html.

ReigningIt. "Women Who Reign: Areeta Wong." Medium, May 22, 2017. https://reigningit.medium.com/women-who-reign-areeta-wong-311abcdf3446.

Unit 10: Jaylen Arnold

"Our Story: Jaylens Challenge." Our Story | Jaylens Challenge. Accessed April 25, 2021. https://jaylenschallenge.org/content/our-story.

Unit 11: Jordan Reeves

"Glitter Blasting Prosthetic Arm Empowers Kids with Disabilities." YouTube, July 24, 2019. https://www.youtube.com/watch?v=oudmlw13lek.

Krasavage, Nicole. "A Girl and Her Glitter-Shooting Prosthetic: 'You Can Do Anything.'" CNN. Cable News Network, February 13, 2017. https://www.cnn.com/2017/02/13/health/jordan-reeves-born-just-right-limb-difference-profile.

Sandack, Emily. amysmartgirls.com/born-just-right-49ba3bac453f.

Made in the USA
Monee, IL
03 May 2026